ROBERT LOUIS STEVENSON'S

The Body-snatcher

Peter Leigh

Published in association with The Basic Skills Agency

Hodder & Stoughton

A MEMBER OF THE HODDER HEADLINE GROUP

Acknowledgements
Cover: Dave Smith
Illustrations: Jim Eldridge
Photograph: Mary Evans Picture Library

Every effort has been made to trace copyright holders of material reproduced in this book. Any rights not acknowledged will be acknowledged in subsequent printings if notice is given to the publisher.

Orders; please contact Bookpoint Ltd, 39 Milton Park, Abingdon, Oxon OX14 4TD. Telephone: (44) 01235 400414, Fax: (44) 01235 400454. Lines are open from 9.00–6.00, Monday to Saturday, with a 24 hour message answering service.
Email address: orders@bookpoint.co.uk

British Library Cataloguing in Publication Data
A catalogue record for this title is available from the British Library

ISBN 0 340 77463 0

First published 2000
Impression number 10 9 8 7 6 5 4 3 2 1
Year   2005 2004 2003 2002 2001 2000

Typeset by GreenGate Publishing Services, Tonbridge, Kent.
Printed in Great Britain for Hodder and Stoughton Educational, a division of Hodder Headline Plc, 338 Euston Road, London NW1 3BH, by Redwood Books, Trowbridge, Wilts

About the Author

Robert Louis Stevenson was born in 1850.
He is one of Scotland's greatest writers.
He had a remarkable life.
He travelled across America
at the time of the Wild West.
He settled in Samoa.
He died there in 1894.

About the Story

Doctors have to know
every part of the body.
They have to know the bones,
the muscles, and the skin.
In the early days of medicine
there was only one way of learning all this.
Dissection!
That means carefully cutting up
dead bodies into parts or sections
to see how they work.

The trouble was
there weren't many bodies to dissect.
In fact there were very few.
People don't like the thought of being
cut up by students when they are dead.

Hospitals began to offer a lot of money
for bodies.
And they didn't ask too many questions
about where they had come from.

This is a story from those times.

I

Fettes was a student.
He was a good student,
and worked hard.
Like many other students
he earned money
by working at the hospital.

He was assistant to the professor.
His job was to look after
the operating theatre and the lecture-room.
He also had to deal with the bodies
for dissection.
They would arrive in the middle of the night.
He would receive them,
and pay for them.
Then he had to divide them up
for the morning's lessons.

The bodies worried Fettes.
Sometimes they looked very fresh.
And the men who brought them
looked evil and suspicious.

But the professor told him
to ask no questions.
'They bring the body,
and we pay the price,'
he used to say.

So Fettes' job was to take what was brought,
to pay the price,
and to look away.

One night he was woken by a knock
on the door.
It was the men with another body.
There was a thin, bright moonshine.
It was bitter cold, windy, and frosty.

They had come later than usual,
and they seemed keen to get away.
Fettes was only half awake
As they emptied the sack onto the slab
he leaned against the wall dozing.
He had to shake himself
to find the money for them.
As he did so

lighted – fell   his eyes lighted on the dead face.

He started.
He took two steps nearer,
with the candle raised.

'God Almighty!' he cried.
'That is Jane Galbraith!'

The men said nothing,
but they shuffled nearer the door.

'I know her, I tell you,' he said.
'She was alive and well yesterday.
It's impossible she can be dead.
It's impossible you should have
got this body fairly.'

'You're mistaken, sir!'
said one of the men.

But the other looked Fettes darkly in the eyes.
He demanded the money on the spot.

Fettes could not mistake the threat
in the man's voice.
He knew he was in danger
if he said another word.
His courage failed him.
He stammered some excuses,
and counted out the sum.

He felt afraid.

4

No sooner were they gone
than he hurried to the body.
It was definitely Jane Galbraith.
He saw, with horror,
that there were marks upon her body.
They were marks of violence.
He was seized with fright.
He ran back to his room.
There he sat for the rest of the night
in a state of panic and fear.

Fettes knew another student,
Wolfe Macfarlane.
He was popular with the other students.
He was clever, and unscrupulous.

unscrupulous –
ruthless and not
caring about other
people

He worked with Fettes.
In fact he had often helped him find bodies.

On that particular morning
Macfarlane arrived earlier than usual.
Fettes heard him,
and met him on the stairs.

He told him what had happened,
and showed him the body.
Macfarlane examined the marks.

'Yes,' he said, with a nod.
'It does look fishy.'

'What should I do?' asked Fettes.

'Do?' repeated the other.
'Don't do anything!
Least said soonest mended, I say.'

Macfarlane thinks it is best to put their worries to the back of their minds.

'Some one might recognise her,' said Fettes.
'She was well known.'

'Well, if anybody does,' said Macfarlane,
'you didn't!
And that's the end of it.
The fact is,
this has been going on for ages now.
Stir up the mud,
and you'll get the professor into trouble,
and yourself.
And me as well, if it comes to that.
What would any of us say in court?
For there's one thing certain –
all our subjects have been murdered.'

'Macfarlane!' cried Fettes.

'Come now!' sneered the other.
'As if you hadn't suspected it yourself.'

'Suspecting is one thing.'

'And proof another.
Yes, I know.
And I'm as sorry as you are
that this has happened.
The next best thing is to say nothing.
That's what I'm going to do.
You do as you wish –
I'm not telling you –
but I think a man of the world
would do as I do.
And I think that is what the professor
would expect of us.
After all, why did he choose us for his
assistants?
Because he didn't want old wives.'

Fettes turned it over in his mind.
The more he thought about it
the more he had to agree.
Macfarlane was right.

So Fettes followed Macfarlane's advice,
and said nothing.
The body of the poor girl was duly dissected.
No-one said anything,
or appeared to recognise her.

a man of the world
– a man with
experience of life

He didn't want
people who would
talk about what they
saw.

They did nothing so
the dissection of
Jane Galbraith's
body went ahead.

II

One day after work,
Fettes went to a local bar.
Macfarlane was there.
He was sitting with a stranger.
He was a small man,
very pale and dark, with coal-black eyes.
His name was Gray.

Gray was rough,
rude and not very
clever.

He was coarse, vulgar, and stupid.
But he seemed to have
some sort of hold over Macfarlane.
He welcomed Fettes.
He ordered him lots of drinks.
Macfarlane had to pay.

'Toddy, order your friend another glass,'
he said. 'I call him Toddy. Toddy Macfarlane.'
And, 'Toddy, jump up and shut the door.'

Then he said, 'Toddy hates me.
Don't you, Toddy?
Oh, yes, Toddy, you do!'

'Don't call me by that confounded name,'
growled Macfarlane.

Gray asks Fettes
whether he has seen
a dissection.

'Listen to him!
Did you ever see the lads play knife?
Toddy would like to do that.
All over my body.'

'We medics have a better way than that,'
said Fettes.
'When we don't like someone,
we dissect them.'

Macfarlane looked up sharply,
as if he had been thinking that very thing.

Gray invited Fettes to join them for dinner.
He ordered a huge feast.
When all was done
he told Macfarlane to settle the bill.

It was late before they went home.
Gray was drunk.
Macfarlane was furious.
He was angry at the money
he had been forced to waste,
and at the insults
he had been forced to swallow.

Next day Macfarlane was absent from class.
Fettes smiled to himself.
Macfarlane must be taking Gray
round all the bars.

When the class was finished,
he went to join them.
But he couldn't find them anywhere.
So he went back to his rooms,
and went to bed early.

At four in the morning
he was woken by a knock.
He went to the door.
It was Macfarlane.
On the ground next to him
was one of those long and ghastly shapes
which he knew so well.

There was a body wrapped in cloth on the ground.

'What?' cried Fettes.
'Have you been out alone?
How did you manage?'

But Macfarlane silenced him roughly.
'Let's just get on with it,' he said.

When they had got the body upstairs,
they laid it on the table.
Macfarlane said,
'You had better look at the face.'

'Why?'

'Just look at the face,' was the only answer.
Fettes felt a strange doubt.
He looked from Macfarlane to the body,
and then back again.

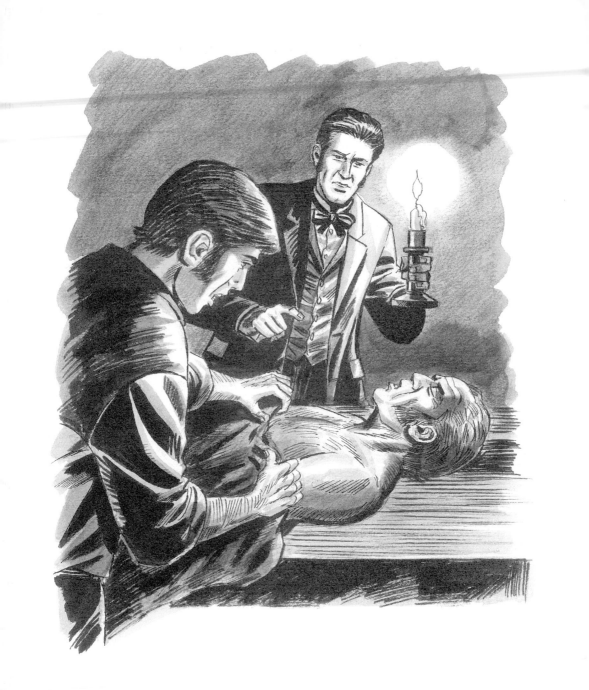

At last, he did as he was asked.
He almost knew
what he was going to see,
and yet the shock was cruel.
There, stiff and naked

sackcloth – a type
of rough material

on that coarse layer of sackcloth,
was Gray.
Fettes was terrified.
He couldn't speak.
He couldn't even look at Macfarlane.

Macfarlane himself spoke first.

'Richardson can have the head.'

Richardson was a student.
He had long wanted a head to dissect.

Fettes still could say nothing.
Macfarlane carried on.
'Talking of business,
you must pay me.
Your accounts must tally.'

The number of
bodies and the
money paid must
add up.

At last Fettes found his voice.
'Pay you!' he cried.
'Pay you for that?'

'Why, yes, of course you must!
By all means you must!
I dare not give it you for nothing.
You dare not take it for nothing.
It would compromise us both.
This is just like Jane Galbraith.
The more things are wrong
the more we must act
as if all were right.
Where does the professor keep his money?'
'There,' answered Fettes hoarsely,
pointing to a cupboard in the corner.

'Give me the key, then,' said the other calmly,
holding out his hand.

Fettes hesitated a moment.
Then he gave Macfarlane the key.
It was done.
There was no going back.

Macfarlane took the key.
He opened the cupboard.
He took some money,
and handed the account-book to Fettes.

They may be found out if they do not act normally.

'Look,' he said, 'I've taken payment.
That's the first step to safety.
You now have to take the second.
Enter the payment in your book,
and then you can defy the devil.'

He will trick
everyone, even the
devil.

The next few seconds
were an agony of doubt for Fettes.
But then he steeled himself.

He hardened himself.

With a steady hand
he entered the date and the amount
in the book.

'And now,' said Macfarlane,
'it's only fair that you should
share in the money.
I've had my share already.'

'Macfarlane,' spoke Fettes at last,
'I have put my neck in a noose to help you.'

'To help me?' cried Macfarlane.
'Oh, come now.
As far as I can see,
you did what you had to.
Suppose I got into trouble,
where would you be?
This Mr Gray is the same thing as
Miss Galbraith.
You can't begin and then stop.
If you begin,
you must keep on beginning.
That's the truth.
No rest for the wicked.'

He was right.
Fettes was trapped.

A feeling of horror
swept over him.

He was overcome with black dismay.

'My God' he cried.
'What have I done?'

16

'My dear fellow,' said Macfarlane.
'What a boy you are!
What harm has come to you?
What harm can come to you
if you hold your tongue?
Listen! In this world
there are two types –
the lions and the lambs.
If you're a lamb,
you'll end up on these tables
like Gray or Jane Galbraith.
If you're a lion,
you'll live and grow rich like me –
or like anyone with any wit or courage.
I know. You're shaken at first.
But my dear fellow, you're clever,
you have pluck.
I like you.
You were born to lead the hunt.
I tell you, three days from now
you'll laugh at all this.'

to have pluck – to be brave

a paid accomplice –
someone who is paid
for their help

And with that Macfarlane left.
Fettes was helpless.
He had become Macfarlane's paid accomplice.
He would have given the world
to have been a little braver earlier on.
It did not occur to him
that he might still be brave.
The secret of Jane Galbraith

The cursed entry in
the account-book is
the money that
Fettes paid and
recorded for Gray's
body.

and the cursed entry in the account-book
closed his mouth.

Hours passed.
The class began to arrive.
The body of the unhappy Gray
was divided up among the students.
No-one said anything.
Richardson was happy with the head.
Fettes began to hope.
Every second brought him closer to safety.

For two days he continued to watch,
with increasing joy.
Before the week was out
it had come true,
exactly as Macfarlane had said.
Nobody said anything about Gray's body.
Fettes was safe.

In time his fears
died. He began to
feel that he had been
brave and he even
felt proud.

He outlived his terrors
and forgot his weakness.
He began to plume himself
upon his courage.
He retold the story in his mind.
His part in it grew bigger and bigger.
He began to be proud
of what he had done.

Of Macfarlane he saw little.
They met, of course, in the class.
They took their orders together from
the professor.
But they avoided any mention of their secret.
Once Fettes whispered to Macfarlane
that he was now a lion,
and no longer a lamb.
But Macfarlane just smiled.

III

But Gray's body didn't last long.
More bodies were needed.
News came that a farmer's wife
had died in a nearby village.
Her body was buried in the churchyard.

Late one afternoon
Fettes and Macfarlane set out to get it.

It was pouring –
a cold, dense, lashing rain.
As they drove towards the village in their
horse and cart
they were like two vultures circling a lamb.

vultures are birds
that will circle round
a weak and dying
creature. They feed
once the animal is
dead.

They stopped once,
to hide their tools in a thick bush
not far from the churchyard.
Then they went on to an inn,
to wait until it was late.
They had a meal and a drink.
They sat in front of the fire
with the rain beating on the window.
They had one drink. Then another.
With each drink
they became more cheerful.

Soon Macfarlane handed a little pile of gold
to Fettes.

'A present,' he said.
'Between friends.'

Fettes pocketed the money.
'You were right,' he cried.
'I was an ass
till I knew you.
You'll make a man of me yet.'

'You don't need it,' said Macfarlane.
'A man? I tell you,
it needed a man
to back me up over Gray.

burly – strong

There are some big, burly cowards
who would have turned sick
at the sight of that body.
But not you –
you kept your head.
I watched you.'

'Well, and why not?' said Fettes.
'It was no affair of mine.

It was an easy
choice between
trouble and pleasing
Macfarlane.

There was only trouble on one side,
and your gratitude on the other.'
And he slapped his pocket
till the gold pieces rang.

He carried on.
'The great thing is not to be afraid.
Now, between you and me,
I don't want to hang –
that's common sense.
But all the rest –
Hell, God, Devil, right, wrong, sin, crime –
well, they may frighten boys,
but men of the world,
like you and me, despise them.
Here's to the memory of Gray!'

By now it was late.
They paid their bill,
and set off.
They deliberately went
in the wrong direction.
When they were clear of the village,
they stopped,
and put out the lamps.
They came back into the village
by a side road.
There was no sound
but the unending pouring of the rain.

It was pitch dark.
They had to pick their way through
the blackness.
Finally, under the dripping trees,
they reached the churchyard.

They didn't want anyone to guess where they were going.

They had to work in darkness,
but they were both used to it,
and powerful with the spade.
After only twenty minutes
they heard a dull rattle on the coffin lid.
They quickly brought it up,
and broke it open.
They wrapped the body in a
dripping sackcloth
and carried to the cart.
They put it on the seat between them.
Then they set off.

They went very carefully,
until they reached the road.
Then they pushed the horse to a good pace
and began to rattle along towards the city.

They had both been wetted to the skin.
Now, as the cart jumped among the deep ruts,

They were holding
the body up between
them.

the thing that stood propped between them
fell now upon one and now upon the other.
At every horrid touch
they had to push it away.

They began to feel
afraid.

It began to tell upon their nerves.

He tried to tell a joke
but he was so afraid
that he didn't really
mean it.

Macfarlane tried to make some joke
about the farmer's wife,
but it came hollowly from his lips.
Still the body bumped from side to side.

The way the head
lies it seems as if it
is alive, comfortable
and trusting.

And now the head would be laid,
as if in confidence, upon their shoulders.
And now the drenching sackcloth
would flap icily about their faces.

Fettes fear grew.

A chill began to creep into the soul of Fettes.
He peered at the bundle.
Somehow it seemed to be larger than at first.
From all over the country-side,
the farm dogs howled as they went past.

An idea took root in Fettes mind.
He began to think

The body had
changed in some
terrible and evil way.

that some unnatural miracle had happened,
that some nameless change had befallen the
dead body,
and that the dogs were howling in fear of it.
He tried to put it to one side,
but it would not go away.
It grew worse and worse, until –
'For God's sake!' he cried.
'For God's sake, let's have a light!'

Macfarlane was affected in the same way.
He stopped the horse,
and got down.
He tried to light the lamp.
The rain still poured down.
It was no easy matter
to make a light in such a world of wet
and darkness.

When at last the flame began to
burn more brightly,
it became possible
for them to see the thing
they had along with them.

The head was
separate from the
body and the
shoulders could be
clearly seen.

riveted – fixed or
fastened

The rain had moulded the rough sacking
to the outlines of the body underneath.
The head was distinct from the trunk,
the shoulders plainly modelled.
Something kept their eyes
riveted upon their ghastly companion.

Macfarlane stood without moving,
holding up the lamp.
A nameless fear was wrapped about Fettes,
like the wet sheet that was wrapped about
the body.
It was a fear that was meaningless,
a horror of what could not be.
But he could not keep it out of his brain.

a nameless fear – a
fear so terrible that it
cannot be described

'That is not a woman,' said Macfarlane, in a
hushed voice.

'It was a woman when we put her in,'
whispered Fettes.

'Hold that lamp,' said the other.
'I must see her face.'

Fettes took the lamp.
Macfarlane untied the fastenings of the sack,
and drew down the cover from the head.
The light fell very clear upon the
dark features and smooth-shaven cheeks
of a face they knew well,
both in life and in their dreams.

A wild yell rang from them.
Each leaped from his own side
into the roadway.
The lamp fell, broke, and went out.
and the horse, startled,
bounded off toward the city at a gallop,
pulling the cart behind it.
Now it had just one occupant –
the body of the dead
and long-dissected Gray!